KT-437-295

Selected by
Robert Hull

Illustrated by
Annabel Spenceley

Thematic Poetry

Animal Poetry
Christmas Poetry
Green Poetry
Sea Poetry

Series editor: Catherine Ellis
Book editor: Cally Chambers
Designer: Derek Lee

First published in 1991 by
Wayland (Publishers) Ltd
61 Western Road, Hove
East Sussex, BN3 1JD, England

British Library Cataloguing in Publication Data

Christmas poetry. – (Thematic poetry)
I. Hull, Robert II. Series
821

ISBN 0-7502-0171-1

Typeset by Kalligraphic Design Ltd, Horley, Surrey. Printed in Italy by G. Canale & C.S.p.A., Turin. Bound in France by A.G.M.

Acknowledgements
Cadbury Ltd for 'Christmas Joy' from *Cadbury's Seventh Book of Children's Poetry* © Cadbury Ltd; David Higham Associates for 'Mistletoe' from *Collected Poems* by Charles Causley (Macmillan); Grafton Books (Harper Collins Publishers) for 'Little Tree' by e e cummings from *Complete Poems 1913-1962*; John Murray (Publishers) for extract from 'Advent 1955' from *Uncollected Poems* by John Betjeman; Peterloo Poets for 'Robin's Round' by U. A. Fanthorpe from *Standing To* (Peterloo Poets, 1985); Peters Fraser and Dunlop Group Ltd for 'Christmas Landscape' from *Selected Poems* by Laurie Lee (Andre Deutsch Ltd); Mrs A.M. Walsh for 'Christmas Tree' by John Walsh from *Poets in Hand* (Penguin Books). 'It's Nice, but what is it?', taken from *Santa Claus is Superman* © 1988 Colin McNaughton. Published in the UK by Walker Books Limited. While every effort has been made to trace the copyright holders, in some cases it has proved impossible. The publishers apologise for this apparent negligence.

Picture Acknowledgements
The publishers wish to thank the following for allowing their illustrations to be reproduced in this book: Bruce Coleman 6 (Reinhard); Chapel Studios 13; Habitat Stores 5; Hutchison 26; Photri 15, 42; Tony Stone Worldwide 9, 10, 20, 25, 29, 30, 35, 38, 45; Topham 19; ZEFA cover (both), 16, 23, 41.

Contents

Introduction

Fancy 'introducing' Christmas. 'Children, this is Christmas.' 'Christmas, these are children.' Really! As if you didn't know Christmas already.

What is it for you that's specially unforgettable? Is it the excitement of going round the shops looking for presents, gazing into decorated windows, wanting nearly everything? Is it decorating the tree, or getting ready for the school nativity play? Singing carols? Opening presents? Is it turkey? Christmas pudding? More pudding?

Perhaps Christmas itself is really a gift – under all those shiny wrappings. Suppose we unwrap Christmas to find out what it is. First we take off the shiny covering of buying and selling, then all that bulky eating and drinking. Next there's a silvery wrapping of trees and presents and cards with robins on, and under that we find beautiful carols and music. Inside the carols and music we can already guess what our gift is. We open it, and find simply – a story about love. A smashing present, guaranteed for at least twenty centuries.

What does Christmas give you? What do you remember about your Christmases? What can you imagine about other people's? Can you even imagine it without the kind of things you've just thought of ? Perhaps it's not so hard to imagine, if you know of people who don't have enough presents, uncles, pudding, crackers, love.

Poets remember their own Christmases, but they also imagine other people's. The robin would be a good Christmas poet if he could talk. He's seen them all.

Mistletoe

Mistletoe new,
Mistletoe old,
Cut it down
With a knife of gold.

Mistletoe green,
Mistletoe milk,
Let it fall
On a scarf of silk.

Mistletoe from
The Christmas oak,
Keep my house
From lightning stroke.

Guard from thunder
My roof-tree
And any evil
That there be.

CHARLES CAUSLEY

little tree

little tree
little silent Christmas tree
you are so little
you are more like a flower

who found you in the green forest
and were you very sorry to come away?
see i will comfort you
because you smell so sweetly

i will kiss your cool bark
and hug you safe and tight
just as your mother would,
only don't be afraid

look the spangles
that sleep all the year in a dark box
dreaming of being taken out and allowed to shine,
the balls the chains red and gold the fluffy threads,

put up your little arms
and i'll give them all to you to hold
every finger shall have its ring
and there won't be a single place dark or unhappy

then when you're quite dressed
you'll stand in the window for everyone to see
and how they'll stare!
oh but you'll be very proud

and my little sister and i will take hands
and looking up at our beautiful tree
we'll dance and sing
'Noel Noel'

e e cummings

Robin's Round

I am the proper
Bird for this season –
Not blessed St Turkey,
Born to be eaten.

I'm man's inedible
Permanent bird.
I dine in his garden,
My spoon is his spade.

I'm the true token
Of Christ the Child-King:
I nest in man's stable,
I eat at man's table,
Through all his dark winters
I sing.

U. A. FANTHORPE

From *Advent 1955*

Last year I sent out twenty yards,
Laid end to end, of Christmas cards
To people that I scarcely know –
They'd sent a card to me, and so
I had to send one back. Oh dear!
Is this a form of Christmas cheer?
Or is it, which is less surprising,
My pride gone in for advertising?
The only cards that really count
Are that extremely small amount
From real friends who keep in touch
And are not rich but love us much.
Some ways indeed are very odd
By which we hail the birth of God.

JOHN BETJEMAN

ME
RR
Y
CHR
IS
TM
AS

Christmas Joy

The audience, chilled from the frosty night
Fumbled into the stuffy hall.
Silver stars clung,
Tinsel was drooped around the crammed room.
They sat, not knowing what to expect
From a group of children wearing old curtains
And tinsel round their heads.
The hall grew warmer,
A light beamed on to a home-made crib.
A cloth was draped over Jesus' worn face.
Backstage everyone was excited,
Except me.
Hot and clammy, I sat in a corner
Waiting for my turn.
I was pushed on to the stage
And blinded.
My angel's costume was crumpled,
My face was numb.
I could see the Headmaster
Lounging in his plastic chair.
He gave a smile,
Urging me to speak.
One eye gave a friendly wink.
It was Christmas.

HELEN ROBINSON (aged 13)

Silly Question

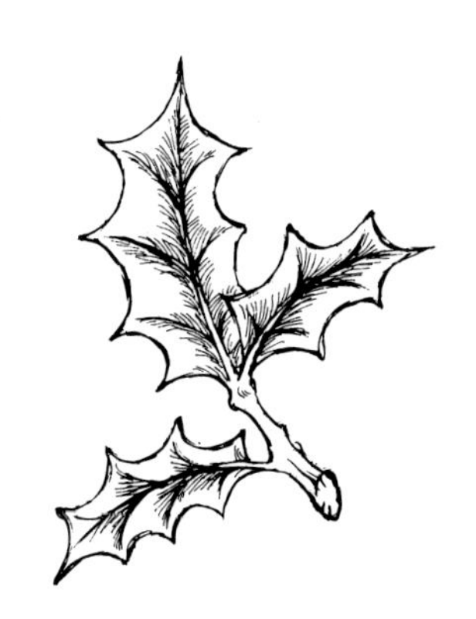

'Why is your pram full of holly?
There should be a baby inside.'

'My baby is noisy and smelly
And the holly's enjoying the ride.'

SUE COWLING

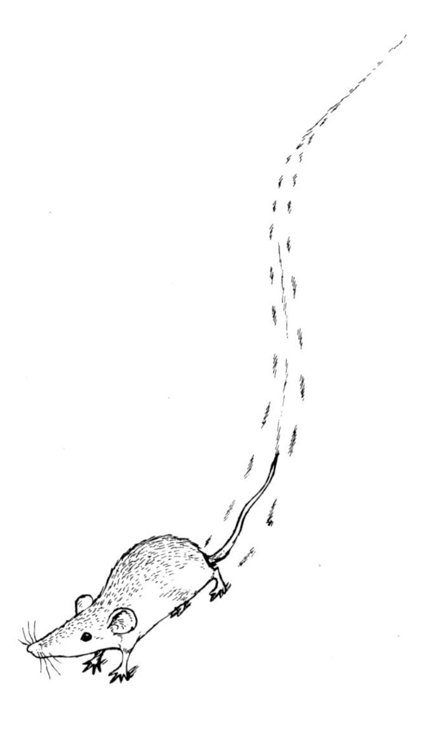

Merry Christmas

I saw on the snow
when I tried on my skis
the track of a mouse
beside some trees.

Before he tunneled
to reach his house
he wrote 'Merry Christmas'
in white, in mouse.

AILEEN FISHER

Xmas

I forgot to send
A card to Jennie –
But the truth about cousins is
There's too many.

I also forgot
My Uncle Joe
But I believe I'll let
That old rascal go.

I done bought
Four boxes now
I can't afford
No more, no how.

So Merrry Xmas,
Everybody!
Cards or no cards
Here's HOWDY!

LANGSTON HUGHES

From *What is the Truth?*

Geese are godly creatures, not just for Christmas show.
At my first note on their bucket, though it's ten degrees below,
Their choir stands in a ring and they lift their throats of snow.

And they carol out their discords, till their tall necks fence me in
With a rusty-shipyard bonging echoing hollow din.
Noël, Noël, they clang to God, which can't be called a sin.

Devil's feet of lizard leather! Wrangling, squirmy necks!
Hissing cauldrons! Haggish witches gabbling out a hex!
It's only the gander warning you from his wives with a threat
of pecks –

The ladies laugh their loony laughter, gossiping together,
Or arguing about a puddle, or a duck's feather.
Or they remember the white seas and the snows of polar weather

And all begin to sing, and stretch up as if to fly
At a sudden vision of icebergs, and they yodel out a cry
That cannons between iron mountains and an iron sky –

But all fall like snow. It is sad, but it must be.
I sit and bare the breast of down, the weight across my knee,
And I'm ankle-deep in the whiteness, and the fluff goes
floating free,

Till the poor body's nude as a babe, except for the neck and head,
The neck in its muff, its ruff of plumes, pretending to be dead,
But the bright eye still open hearing every word that's said,

And the beak that worked so hard at the world, and sang to
me so strong,
Holding carefully silent the plump tip of its tongue
Lest it spoil our Christmas Feast with any whisper of wrong.

TED HUGHES

The Oxen

CHRISTMAS EVE, and twelve of the clock.
'Now they are all on their knees,'
An elder said as we sat in a flock
By the embers in hearthside ease.

We pictured the meek mild creatures where
They dwelt in their strawy pen,
Nor did it occur to one of us there
To doubt they were kneeling then.

So fair a fancy few would weave
In these years! Yet, I feel,
If someone said on Christmas Eve,
'Come; see the oxen kneel

'In the lonely barton by yonder coomb
Our childhood used to know,'
I should go with him in the gloom,
Hoping it might be so.

THOMAS HARDY

From *A Christmas Package*

My stocking's where
He'll see it – there!
One-half a pair.

The tree is sprayed,
My prayers are prayed,
My wants are weighed.

I've made a list
Of what he missed
Last year. I've kissed

My father, mother,
Sister, brother;
I've done those other

Things I should
And would and could.
So far, so good.

DAVID McCORD

Reindeer Report

Chimneys: colder.
Flightpaths: busier.
Driver: Christmas (F)
Still baffled by postcodes.

Children: more
And stay up later.
Presents: heavier.
Pay: frozen.

Mission in spite
Of all this
Accomplished.

U. A. FANTHORPE

From *Christmas Landscape*

Tonight the wind gnaws
With teeth of glass,
The jackdaw shivers
in caged branches of iron,
the stars have talons.

There is hunger in the mouth
of vole and badger,
silver agonies of breath
in the nostril of the fox,
ice on the rabbit's paw.

Tonight has no moon,
no food for the pilgrim;
the fruit tree is bare,
the rose bush a thorn
and the ground bitter with stones.

But the mole sleeps, and the hedgehog
lies curled in a womb of leaves,
the bean and the wheat-seed
hug their germs in the earth
and the stream moves under the ice.

Tonight there is no moon,
but a new star opens
like a silver trumpet over the
dead.
Tonight in a nest of ruins
the blessed babe is laid.

LAURIE LEE

The Barn

'I am tired of this barn!' said the colt.
'And every day it snows.
Outside there's no grass any more
And icicles grow on my nose.
I am tired of hearing the cows
Breathing and talking together.
I am sick of these clucking hens.
I *hate* stables and winter weather!'

'Hush, little colt,' said the mare,
'And a story I will tell
Of a barn like this one of ours
And the wonders that there befell.
It was weather much like this,
And the beasts stood as we stand now
In the warm good dark of the barn –
A horse and an ass and a cow.'

'And sheep?' asked the colt. 'Yes, sheep,
And a pig and a goat and a hen.
All of the beasts of the barnyard,
The usual servants of men.
And into their midst came a lady
And she was cold as death,
But the animals leaned above her
And made her warm with their breath.

'There was her baby born
And laid to sleep in the hay,
While music flooded the rafters
And the barn was as light as day.
And angels and kings and shepherds
Came to worship the babe from afar,
But we looked at him first of
all creatures
By the bright strange light of a star!'

ELIZABETH COATSWORTH

Christmas at Sea

The sheets were frozen hard, and they cut the naked hand;
The decks were like a slide, where a seaman scarce could stand;
The wind was a nor'wester, blowing squally off the sea;
And cliffs and spouting breakers were the only things a-lee.

They heard the surf a-roaring before the break of day;
But 'twas only with the peep of light we saw how ill we lay.
We tumbled every hand on deck instanter, with a shout,
And we gave her the maintops'l, and stood by to go about.

All day we tacked and tacked between the South Head and the North;
All day we hauled the frozen sheets, and got no further forth;
All day as cold as charity, in bitter pain and dread,
For very life and nature we tacked from head to head.

We gave the South a wider berth, for there the tide-race roared;
But every tack we made we brought the North Head close aboard:
So's we saw the cliffs and houses, and the breakers running high,
And the coastguard in his garden, with his glass against his eye.

The frost was on the village roofs as white as ocean foam;
The good red fires were burning bright in every 'longshore home;
The windows sparkled clear, and the chimneys volleyed out;
And I vow we sniffed the victuals as the vessel went about.

Sheets: *ropes used to adjust the sails*

The bells upon the church were rung with a mighty jovial cheer;
For it's just that I should tell you how (of all days in the year)
This day of our adversity was blessed Christmas morn,
And the house above the coastguard's was the house where
I was born.

O well I saw the pleasant room, the pleasant faces there,
My mother's silver spectacles, my father's silver hair;
And well I saw the firelight, like a flight of homely elves,
Go dancing round the china-plates that stand upon the shelves.

And well I knew the talk they had, the talk that was of me,
Of the shadow on the household and the son that went to sea;
And O the wicked fool I seemed, in every kind of way,
To be here and hauling frozen ropes on blessed Christmas Day.

They lit the high sea-light, and the dark began to fall.
'All hands to loose topgallant sails,' I heard the captain call.
'By the Lord, she'll never stand it,' our first mate, Jackson, cried.
... 'It's the one way or the other, Mr. Jackson,' he replied.

She staggered to her bearings, but the sails were new and good,
And the ship smelt up to windward just as though she
understood.
As the winter's day was ending, in the entry of the night
We cleared the weary headland, and passed below the light.

And they heaved a mighty breath, every soul on board but me,
As they saw her nose again pointing handsome out to sea;
But all that I could think of, in the darkness and the cold,
Was just that I was leaving home and my folks were growing old.

ROBERT LOUIS STEVENSON

Two Christmas Riddles

I have two waists
and one noise
in my lifetime.

I have a hat
that I can't put on,
and when I scatter,
I bring laughter.

NICOLA PELLOW
(aged 11)

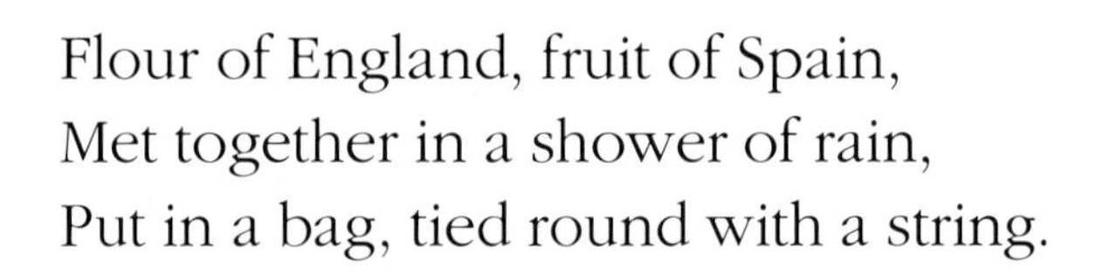

Flour of England, fruit of Spain,
Met together in a shower of rain,
Put in a bag, tied round with a string.

If you tell me this riddle,
I'll give you a ring.

ANON

Christmas at our House

The Christmases at our house
Aren't like the pictures I've seen
On calendars and Christmas cards
Where all is joy serene,
Where red-faced husbands kiss their wives
Beneath sprigs of mistletoe
And fat little angels sing carols
And it always seems to snow.
For a start my Dad starts moaning
Before he's even out of bed
And Elvis, my brother, starts screaming
When his Action Man loses his head.
And Ann won't touch her turkey
And Elvis starts calling her names
And Dad overdoes the brandy
And the pudding bursts into flames.

Auntie May starts singing long, sad hymns
And the mongrel is sick on the mat
While Uncle George gets merry
On just three glasses of sherry
And spills custard all over the cat.
After tea we play disorganized games
And Gran faints away in her chair
And the games always end in tears and sulks
Because Elvis will never play fair.
Sharron falls out with her boyfriend,
Tina stops talking to hers,
Then we have to call the fire brigade
When Tom's head gets stuck in the stairs.
I breathe a sigh of relief when midnight arrives
And the relations all disappear
Because I know for certain that Christmas Day
Won't be round for another whole year.

GARETH OWEN

It's Nice, But What Is It?

Oh, thank you! How kind of you!
Just what I needed!
A blue one with knobs on!
How you have succeeded,
In making my Christmas,
In making my day,
I'm so overwhelmed,
What more can I say?
You shouldn't have bothered,
It must have been dear!
Although there is something
On which I'm not clear –
Its springs are just super,
The fringe on top dandy.
The rocket propulsion
Will come in right handy.
Its drumlins are perfect,
The doobries just right,
The bucket seats comfy,
The lights not too bright.
It's got rudders that shudder
And bloopers that bleep,
Head-rests that rest heads –
It can't have been cheap!
It's a beautiful gift
And its finish exquisite,
Though I have been thinking –
It's nice, but what is it?

COLIN McNAUGHTON

Woman Going to Christmas Party

Now that the babysitter's here,
and the kids in their p.j.s
are hypnotised by Snoopy's Christmas Show,
I can take my hair-rollers out
and put some glitter on my eyelids.
Unfortunately, my youngest puked
on the shoulder of my party-dress,
so I've borrowed a sequined shawl
from next-door and added extra perfume.
Beside the phone, I've left a list
of dos-and-don'ts and a number where,
if all else fails, I can be reached.
Chuck is outside warming up the engine;
but now for the fun part:
digging the car out of a snow-drift.

JULIE O'CALLAGHAN

Gift with the Wrappings Off

Oh, what can you do with a Christmas pup
In a little apartment three flights up?
He prowls.

And whenever the landlord happens by
With a 'Rent's due!' gleam in his fishy eye,
He howls!

Or whenever you dress for a hurry date,
With a frantic prayer that you won't be late,
He 'helps'!

Or when guests sit down in the rocking chair
And neglect to see if a tail is there,
He yelps;

And if you protest that he isn't hurt
And call him out from beneath your skirt,
He balks.

Or perhaps there's rain, or a two-foot snow,
Or it's three *a.m.* – then he's got to go
For walks!

And the place you pick for his bed at night
Is the one sure place that he doesn't quite
Approve.

Oh, what can you do with a Christmas pup
In a little apartment three flights up?
Move?

MARY ELIZABETH COUNSELMAN

The Christmas Tree

They chopped her down in some far wood
A week ago,
Shook from her dark green spikes her load
Of gathered snow,
And brought her home at last, to be
Our Christmas show.

A week she shone, sprinkled with lamps
And fairy frost;
Now, with her boughs all stripped, her lights
And spangles lost,
Out in the garden there, leaning
On a broken post,

She sighs gently ... Can it be
She longs to go
Back to that far-off wood, where green
And wild things grow?
Back to her dark green sisters, standing
In wind and snow?

JOHN WALSH

Biographies

John Betjeman was the Poet Laureate before Ted Hughes. He was knighted Sir John Betjeman, mainly for his poetry, but also because of his enthusiasm for the British heritage.

Charles Causley was born in Cornwall, where he still lives. He was in the Royal Navy, then was a schoolteacher for twenty-five years.

Elizabeth Coatsworth was born in Buffalo, New York, USA in 1893. She travelled a great deal as a child, and later wrote poems for adults and children. Her most popular book for children is called *The Cat Who Went to Heaven*.

Sue Cowling is originally from Merseyside but now lives in Shropshire. She started writing poems only four years ago. She has two children and numerous pets, and these supply her with lots of ideas.

e e cummings wrote his name just like that. He was a famous American poet who used interesting ways of writing his poems on the page and experimented with unexpected punctuation.

U. A. Fanthorpe was born in Kent in 1929. She went to Oxford and then into schoolteaching. After being Head of English at a school for several years, she decided to work as a clerk/receptionist in a hospital in Bristol. She has now won several prizes for her poetry.

Aileen Fisher is an American poet who has written lots of fine poetry for children. Her best-known book of poems is *In the Woods, in the Meadow, in the Sky*, which was published in 1965.

Thomas Hardy (1840–1927) was a famous novelist and poet. He lived nearly all his long life in Dorset. He is one of the greatest English poets.

Langston Hughes (1902–67) has written stories, plays and novels, as well as several books of poems. He is especially remembered for capturing, in his writing, the experience of black people in the USA.

Ted Hughes was born in Yorkshire. In 1984 he was made Poet Laureate. He has written many books for adults and for children. One of the best-known books of poems for children is *Season Songs*.

Laurie Lee was born in Gloucestershire. When he was nineteen he walked to London, and then travelled on foot through Spain where he was caught up in the Civil War.

David McCord, an American poet, was born in 1897. He has written many books about many things – art, education, medicine and history – but he is best known for his light verse, and especially his poems for children.

Colin McNaughton studied illustration at the Royal College of Art. He illustrated many books for children before he wrote his first book of children's verse, *There's An Awful Lot Of Weirdos In Our Neighbourhood.*

Julie O'Callaghan was born in Chicago, USA in 1954, and now lives in Dublin. She writes for adults and children. A book of poems for children, *Taking My Pen for a Walk*, was published in 1988.

Gareth Owen has written plays, novels and stories for children, as well as several plays and musicals for adults which he both acts in and directs.

Nicola Pellow wrote her Christmas riddle in about 1970, when she was in the first year of secondary school.

Helen Robinson, from Brandeston Hall School in Suffolk, was thirteen when she wrote her Christmas poem for the Cadbury Poetry Competition.

Robert Louis Stevenson (1850–94) studied engineering and then law at Edinburgh University. He wrote poetry as well as travel and adventure books. His book *A Child's Garden of Verses* is a favourite with many children. He went to live in Samoa in 1888, and he died there.

John Walsh (1911–1972) was born in Brighton, went to London University to study English, and then became a schoolmaster. He wrote several books, and many of his poems for children were broadcast on BBC Radio for Schools. He lived in East Sussex all his life.

Index of first lines